**The Urbana Free Library**

To renew: call 217-367-4057
or go to *urbanafreelibrary.org*
and select "My Account"

# Jellyfish

**by Grace Hansen**

ABDO
OCEAN LIFE
Kids

**abdopublishing.com**

Published by Abdo Kids, a division of ABDO, PO Box 398166, Minneapolis, Minnesota 55439.

Printed in the United States of America, North Mankato, Minnesota.

102014

012015

 THIS BOOK CONTAINS
RECYCLED MATERIALS

Photo Credits: Glow Images, iStock, Science Source, Shutterstock, Thinkstock, © Nicholas Doumani / CC-BY-ND-2.0 p.18

Production Contributors: Teddy Borth, Jennie Forsberg, Grace Hansen

Design Contributors: Laura Rask, Dorothy Toth

Library of Congress Control Number: 2014943718

Cataloging-in-Publication Data

Hansen, Grace.

Jellyfish / Grace Hansen.

p. cm. -- (Ocean life)

ISBN 978-1-62970-709-9 (lib. bdg.)

Includes index.

1. Jellyfishes--Juvenile literature.    I. Title.

593.5--dc23

2014943718

# Table of Contents

# Jellyfish

Jellyfish live in oceans around the world. They mostly live near **coasts**.

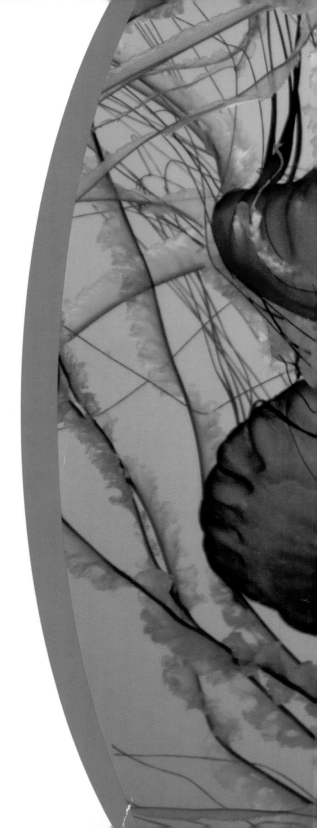

5

Jellyfish can be many
colors. They come in
many shapes and sizes.

7

The arctic lion jellyfish is the biggest. It can reach lengths of 120 feet (37 m)!

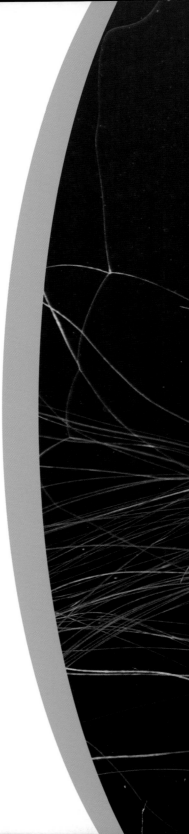

9

A jellyfish's body is called a **bell**. It has a mouth. It has **tentacles** and **oral arms**.

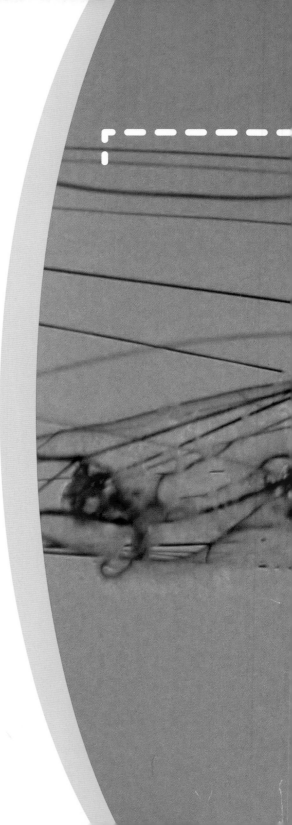

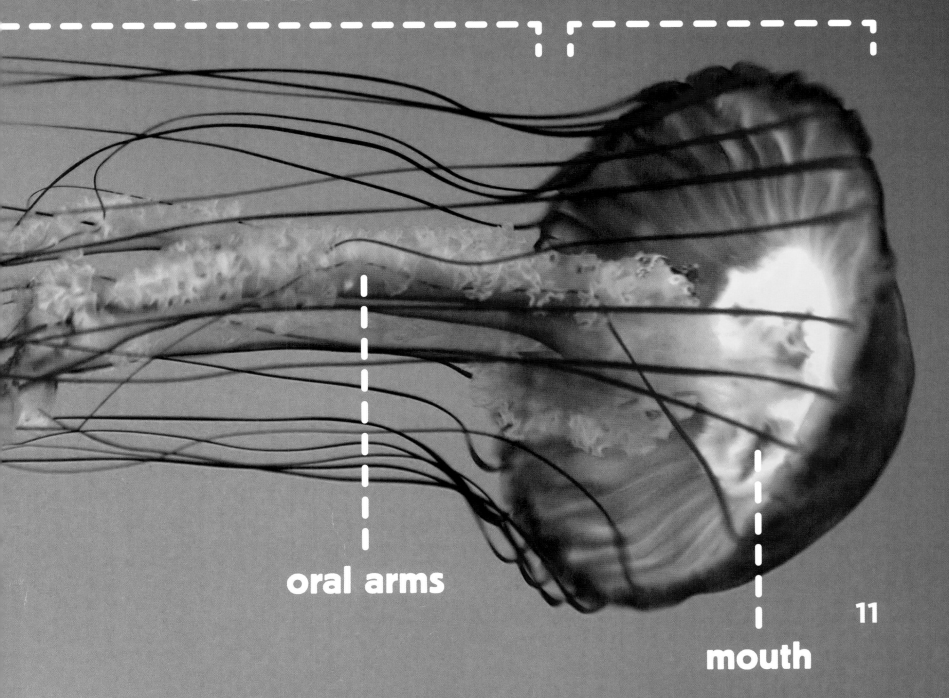

tentacles

bell

oral arms

mouth

11

Jellyfish move slowly.

Some push water out

of their mouths to move.

13

## Food and Eating

Jellyfish **tentacles** catch food. The tentacles sting **prey**.

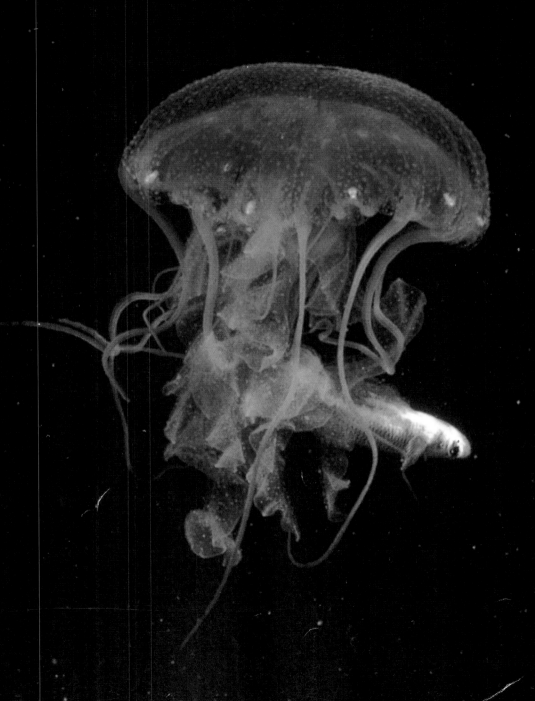

15

The stings are **venomous**.

The venom **paralyzes prey**.

**Oral arms** push food into the mouth.

Jellyfish eat **plankton**.

Big jellyfish will eat fish,

shrimp, and more.

18

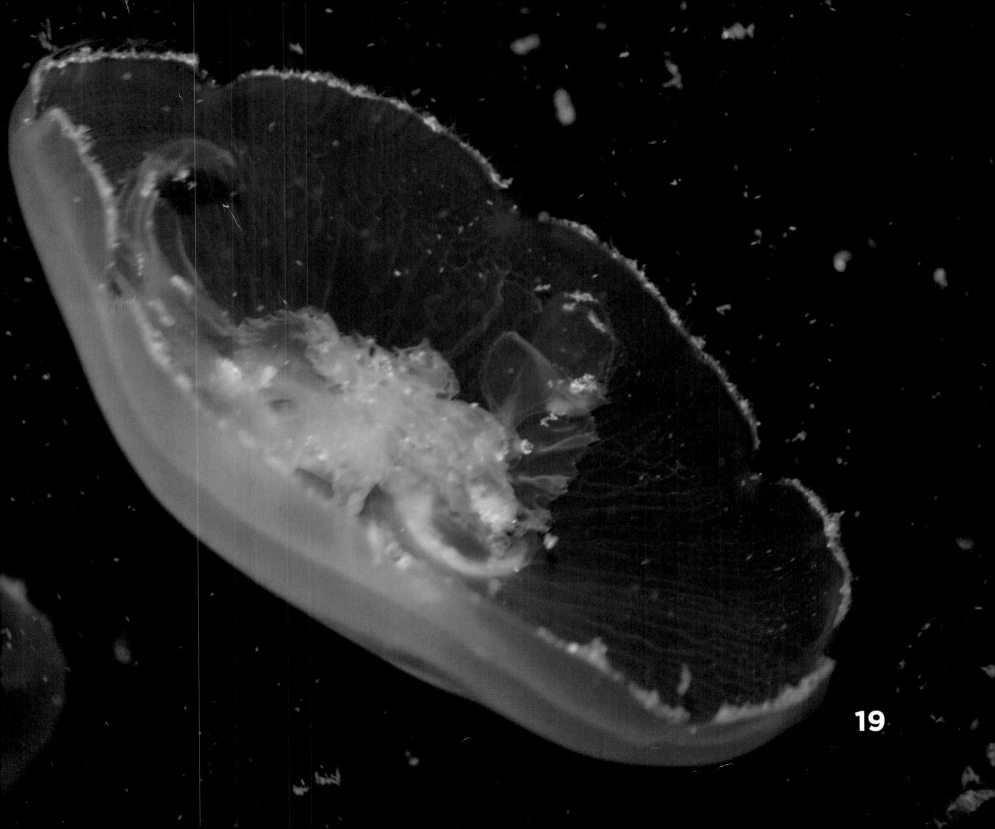

19

## Baby Jellyfish

Jellyfish lay eggs.

Young jellyfish look

very different from adults.

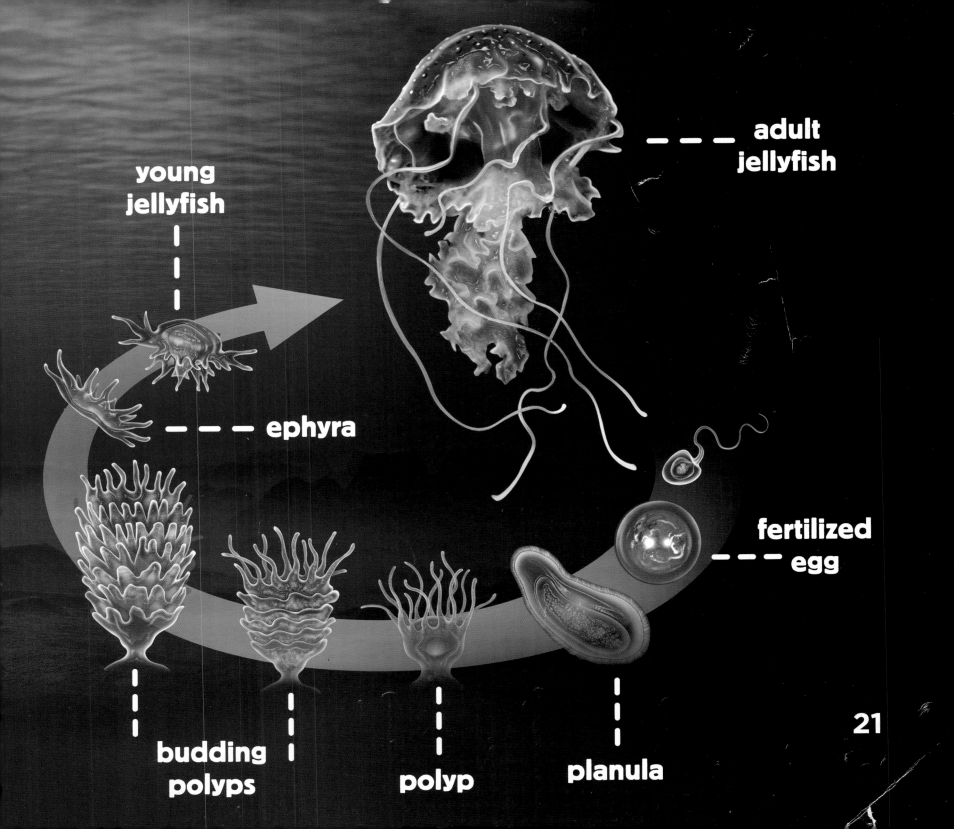

young
jellyfish

adult
jellyfish

ephyra

fertilized
egg

budding
polyps

polyp

planula

21

# More Facts

- Jellyfish are also called "jellies" because they are not really fish.

- There are around 1,500 known species of jellyfish.

- Jellyfish were alive long before the dinosaurs.

# Glossary

**bell** – the bell-shaped body of a jellyfish.

**coast** – land near an ocean.

**oral arm** – a jellyfish usually has four. Located around the mouth and used for feeding. They are thicker than tentacles.

**paralyze** – to cause a loss of motion or feeling in a part of the body.

**plankton** – very small animals that drift through the ocean.

**prey** – an animal hunted or killed for food.

**tentacle** – a slender, flexible arm used to sting prey.

**venomous** – containing venom. Venom is poisonous.

# Index

## abdokids.com

Use this code to log on to abdokids.com and access crafts, games, videos, and more!

Abdo Kids Code:
OJK7099